HOW RICH ARE YOU

Are You Listening

LUCRETIA RITSERT

Brilliant Books Literary
137 Forest Park Lane Thomasville
North Carolina 27360 USA

Listening to the sound of flowing water

My flowers at my home

My artwork

The Rainbow in Bahama

The home I grew up in

Condo in Bahamas coral reef

I Lucretia Ritsert am a artist, music lover, write and sew. Two years and a half I attend art school and received a certificate of merit and an award for drawing, water coloring and sculptor. Some of my art work was hung in a cafe where I once worked and everyone love them. These things I owe to my mother and father. I live in the east of the United States.

I sat in church one Sunday as the Priest ended his Homily by saying "how rich are you' I thought that made my day, because my richness come from the strength I have in God.

Rich was what I had as we grow up, it do not mean always money. I had everything love from my mother, father, brothers and sisters. We also own our home that my father built, contained four bedrooms, dining room, kitchen, living room, bath room, back porch, front porch and a long hallway with upstairs. There was a large front yard with very trees that shade for the summer. There were many flowers on one side of our home my father love his flowers, the ones I remember the most were Iris's, Sunflowers and rose bushes.

There were other trees we could eat the fruit like apples, Bose pears, walnuts, hickey nuts and persimmons. There was vine that grow long and had berries my father build a fence that was tall so he they would not be on the ground, they were like grapes [stuffiness) but outside was not as soft but thicker.

Our garden was very large with lime beans, string beans, beets, white and sweet potatoes, lettie, collard greens, salad greens, turnip greens, which the bottom was white and I would pull up and eat right from the ground, they were so good we had everything plus kale, carrots, tomatoes, watermelons and please don't forget the butterbeans.

For the surrounding area about a mile west of us there were neighbors. One as I remember clearly they were husband and wife, there was to cross over railroad track their home sit in the middle of all this land, very large yard all around. From our house to their was a hill with many trees at the bottom was a pond and I would go fishing and there was also a spring, the water was cold and clear. This is where the husband show me how to fish it was so great, nice and peaceful, the surrounding was wonderful. Writing this story when I was young life was good to me to have God at a very age, still today is one of my best friends I can talk to him any time and place. For me this is my Richness.

I grew up in a small town in Virginia, we lived in a very large house. Our back yard were barns, Hen houses [chickens] where I feed them also takes their eggs in side our home. It was filled with woods and untouched farmland, also landscape which was used for decorative Planting. My sister and I used some parts for making our play houses, we would play for hours until our Father call saying, it time to come home. Now kids say there is nothing to do, they have to be some place checking out the computer. We made our own fun many times there were no TV to look at only a radio for listen, books or magazine like Times to read.

A station that had a frighten story 000 h the shadow known and stellar Dallas. I remember listen to the radio on Saturday morning do not the name of the show but, they always talk about New York. The subject was grand center station [train station] when I came to Philadelphia to live after getting a job, married and became a mother. One of my brother lives in Connecticutt. And was also married, my daughter and I plain a trip to visited him. We took the train in Philadelphia I found we had to change in New York City at grand central station "'that was a dream come true for me. Walking into that station, it took me back when I hear them talking about this station, all the people going difference places, we had to change trains for the new English states, it was great joy in the afternoon and away my daughter and I contained on, my brother meet us at the station. We had a wonderful time with his family. I will never forget his home, it was at one time a church which they turn into a lovely home it was just beautiful.

As one jazz singer once said fun is what one do when listing to some good Jazz. Fun. My brother that lived in Connecticut own a Antique

Shop, it was large also lots of items, of course they were older than me [smile]. We would go with him sometime to see what and how he selects them, he also would go to three places a day. I really enjoy doing this with him, some of the places were like being in the country, being the area for many years he knew everyone. Telling stories about the people and the surrounding towns it gave me an understanding of his life away from home Virginia.

Talking about fun he was a brother that was full of fun love to party and telling many jokes and would make you laugh about everything just love being around him. One evening we went to a club he often attend [like cheers] where everyone knew his name. He was not one of those brothers that told you what you should be doing every ten minutes. He loves me for who I was, a great sister.

I under stood that at a very early age.

There are never two brothers that think the same and that why if you have more than one brother, you will be able to see the difference.

My mother once told me to be true to myself and you would have many friends, she also said to know them very well. She was such a spiritual person, many times she led me to help other people. What a wonderful feeling I had it made me stronger and thankful for the little things in life.

God is speaking to us now, do what he is saying pay attend to the spirit and your heart the Holy Spirit is always with us. Do not change your heart; come Holy Spirit.

Sundays is when we gather with our brothers and sisters [church family]. Forgiving. Rich in Christ our Lord that is where it all begins. We must use what God has given us keep your faith be not afraid I will be with you until the end of the earth.

He says also to guard your tongue to speak and the power to save us all, make us your Peace.

There were many times I went to my home in Va. and stayed with my brother we had lots of good times he love going out to dinner I all ways stay a week, we would out about three times while visiting him. He was like a history book the stories were when he was in the army. Everyone in our town, plus other towns knew him. He did not own a car but on the weekend he would be everywhere. [smile]. He was a great person would do anything for you, also it was good to be around him and love to hear him laugh. He would often come and visited me and my daughter.

I remember this one time my sister, my husband and I went to visited him in the evening we would set out side in early fall we had a Honey Suckle bush along the fence and when the wind came along you could smell the aroma from the Honeysuckle [if only one could put it in bottle] it was wonderful. We would be out for hours some time and we would have a fire going. There would laughter, talking, eating and often napping with blankets wrap around us to keep us very warm. We all had a great time spending this great time with family.

One time I recorded our counteraction, often playing it back and remember what a wonderful evening [smile].

Letter from a friend,

I am writing to say how much I care for you, and to say how much I want you to know me better.

When you awake this morning I exploded a brilliant sunrise through your window hoping to get your attention, but you rushed off without noticing.

Later, I noticed you were walking with some friends, so I bathed you in warm sunshine and perfumed the air with nature's sweet scent, and still you didn't notice me. As you pass by I shouted to you in a thunderstorm and painted a beautiful rainbow in the sky and you didn't even look. In the evening I spilled moonlight onto your face and sent a cool breeze to rest you as you sleep, I watched over you and shared your thoughts, but you were unaware that I was so near.

I have chosen you and hope you will talk to me soon, until than I will remain near. I am your friend and love you very much.

Your friend, Jesus

All my adult life I have been helping family, after my divorced it was my daughter and l, we live nicely in a large city for years, something like from 1969 to 1989. I had six brothers at times two of them were having problems with women I was helping them by saying to put stilly things a side and move on with their lives. Than when one brother became very ill was there when he needed me. This hurt me for a long time, he was the that help me after high school.

When he passed it taught me to look out for myself. He always talks about returning to our home after he would retire but, that day never came. My plain after his death was. I will never be a rich lady [by money that is] but having a strong faith and believing in God and myself I would be all right. I help many people because of whom I have become. When I sent my daughter to college she did well, I help her to received a good education and guided her in the right way for the working world. Now she has a great job and I am proud of her.

I remarried in 1989, my husband and I brought a home in New Jersey there we begin our wonderful life together. We did lots of traveling also he was my best friend. We help each at other at low and high times in our time of married. He was a wonderful and understanding person. God gave me the understanding I needed at the same time. I cry often because I lost my husband in 2007, I know he is in a better place, God knows best.

I am bless in many ways, there has been a great number of wonderful people in my life that help me when I needed them. Each week is a good one because I begin with understanding that God is there for me. I live my life so it will show in what I do. [When I was a little girl we would say let shine, let it shine?]. [smile]

I sat in the church one Sunday, as the Priest ended his Homily by saying How rich are you "I thought that made day because my richness come from the strength I have in God. Rich was what I had as we grow up. It does not mean always money. We had everything like love from our mother and father 'sisters and brothers.

I grew up in a small town in Virginia, backyard were barns, hen housie [chicken] there were lots of them. I had to feed them every day and also go around to get their eggs. The land was filled with woods and untouched farmland, landscapes which was very comforting. My sister and I used some parts for making our play house, we would play for hours now kids say there is nothing to do their fun is playing on computers. We made our own fun. There was no TV to look at we only had a radio to listing, books to read or magazine like Times. We listen to the Shander knows. Stelladaldas they were frighten oooh.

I remember listen to the radio do not know the name of show but it came on Saturday morning. The subject was Grand Central Station [train station that was large] when I came to Phila. To live after getting a Job, married and became a mother. One of my brothers lived in Conn, and married my daughter and I plain a trip to visited him taking a train in Phila… I found out going to Conn. we had to change in New York at Grand Central Station that was a dream come true for me. I never dream walking into that station seeing aII those people going different places. In New York it was [great joy in the afternoon] that was one of my big Dreams. We changed train and away my daughter and I contained on to see my brother, he meet us at the station. We had a wonderful time with him and family. I will never forget that trip he was such a fun person too be around. He home at one time was a church which had was made into loving place to live. July and of 2012 was the first going back to New York to see what happen to Grand Central Station. I found out around sometime in early Seventh [70s] trains going to New England no longer had to change in New York.

Grand Central Terminal was design for trains to go local as I found my way to see my familiar place in 21st century year 2012. I took pictures from the outside, once I get inside the pleasant was all mines on each side as you walk in there were cafes too your left and right. This was up stairs I begin taking pictures and remember how I had seen it in the late sixty. There were also lots of people as it was then plus more, downstairs information was giving to travels as they made their way to their destination. Many shops, a book store and lots of eaties. I found out later on the top floor is a huge restaurant that took up the whole space. A good thing I must return and make another day. Going to New York on Saturday for me to put a new face to my childhood fantasy, turnout to be a wonderful thing. It was just as I picture it to be but more updated. The very great thing I saw Minnie and Mickie Mouse also their friends on Time Square and 42nd street. Wonderful day not too hot great time to see New York. The day ended very well. Stores I went into were Saks Fifth Ave, Ann Taylor and Macys my three stores (love. Bryant Park nice place to be on that sunny day, also being with family or reading a good book. Talking about reading there is large New York Public Library.

God gave us the power to listen when we are still it's all around us, too hear is one of God's blessing he gave to us we all have it. Strong women that gave understanding in my life when I was young my mother with her Christian way of life. My history teacher from high school, my principle from my elementary and she was our neighbor, Mrs. Mary McLeod Bethune I meet when I was at my neighbor home she unstond the children of color, Mrs. O. Turner an artist that owner her hat store. Mrs. Pines head of our new paper in high school also three Priest and one Pastor, men that gave vision of Faith. Going on a retreat in Pa. for a long weekend was a great way for me to learn more about my religion. Meeting at one of the churches taking a school bus, had not rode on a school bus in many years. I am my mother daughter, arrived at Dominican House safe that afternoon. All of Sisters were very helpful to register us and received our room number. After doing this and putting away our things it was time for dinner. Evening Mass was held at 7'30 by Father Theodore Welsh C.P.. He was outstanding. He spoke about 'Fear is usefulness' but trust in the further which is God.

The next morning before breakfast we had prayer which was a good to talk with other people that attend the retreat. Rosary was held at 10:45, I had not attended one for a while so I felt like I should go, so I did. The Chapel was full I understand the Rosary much better now.

Father Ted did the prayer Mass Luke 19'6-10, Jeuse came in Zaccheaeeslife. This was good for me because my mother read this in summer bible class I always like this story. He also talk about may the passion of Jesus Christ be always be in hearts ,God is 'I am' the bread of life, by this time it was lunch , what a great morning 1:45. Our quiet time was to check out the gift shops, library, and books sale. Lot of flowers, cards, some of the flowers were made by the Nuns that were there, it begin to rain but that was ok I walk to the hug garage where their other items. The grounds was very large and also very lovely with lots of trees.

We had to go and hear a story by sister Pat her subject 'Mary'. Mary the mother of Jeuse Mary being like a real mother like, cleaning floors carry water as she was carry a child and she felt being a child before birth. This sister Pat was very good as if you were school again [smile]. In the Chapel soft music was playing for 20 minutes, we all did prayer and gave thanks for the small things in life. Reading were small from the sisters they thanks the Angles, family, church and friends. Angles are real you know they bless us all the time and love each one of us.

On Sunday was a very re-joyful day breakfast was very large, this was our last day. Talking with all the ladies I had met and saying the whole weekend was a joy, after lunch Mass was held at 12:30 I was one of the Eucharist Ministers this made me feel wonderful, making someone else fell great or wonderful or thankful this also ended my weekend with a big small on my face. We had a safe trip home, it was also good to see my lovely husband and he was glad to see me.

After the passing of my brother I begin to travel, the first place was the Caribbean the wonderful islands of St Maarten/Sr. Martin this was a great trip. I travel on the airline Pan Am airplane this was a very large carrier, with three rows of seats it felt as if you were setting in someone large living room. [KLM] what a plane."

After arriving in St. Maarten all the people was so warm and friendly to talk with also helpful in many ways showing you around the Island. I was there for a week, a girl friend I know lived there six months out of a year she was a singer [Jazz] the very best.

While I was there someone suggest that taking a trip on a boat to one of the other smaller Islands could be nice so I did with some other people. This was a great sighing ride about four to five minutes. The name of the Island was 'Anguilla' what a Place. Every one enjoyed the day. Some stayed and others tour the Island like I did it was enjoyable. My tour was with a Cab driver he was tour guide talked about the whole Island, that looked like a Island not a large city.

There one hotel on the island and the front was clear water [white] I could have stayed there for the rest of my vacation the people was so friendly, plus the memories will last me a life time, now is the time I would to return. What a lesson was learned from being at this island for a day trip well done.

To heal for me is having one friend I can laugh and talk about life how I miss not going to visited my great friend. He had faith and understands that god was there for the both of us.

Positive attitude is what I learn to have believed, pray about your problems for a change when you are at the altar and leave it there. The lord takes care of the rest.

WEDDING

Wedding are nice, my husband and I was visited to one in [1999] to Mexico City in our conversation we were asking our self if we should go,1 said why not after reaching a time in your life one don't get a change to visited to a wedding out of the country, I said lets go for it and we did. A friend of our son was to married a young lady and she was from Mexico City. Our friend said we should come because the only thing we could pay a small air fare and the rooms were very cheat. We did not have to pay anything for food because that was taken care by the young lady parents. We went and flight was good arriving about 2 pm, taking a cab ride to hotel at 3'30, after checking into our room it was nice side and the view was also good. They had put our plains in our room before we arrived so we knew what to look forward for the long weekend.

We meet them in the Hospitably Room with other friends and family. There were all this food and drinks making ourselves compatible with laughing and talking until 11:30 pm.

Saturday

Saturday morning we all meet for breakfast after a great meal of anything you would want, the talking was maybe we should all go shopping. Taking a taxicab down town for 3 hours this was something to see not like shopping back home [in the states].

Returning to Hospitality Room for lunch and talking about trip our shopping. This went well, we all went to room to relax for the 9pm wedding.

WEDDING

The wedding was at 9pm, at the end of each Pew there was a candle, also flowers the church was very small but beautiful reminded me of a Greed Orthodox back in the states. The wedding Groom and Bride came out side to sign the married license with their parents, after ward we all went in a taxicab to the restaurant for dinner. Setting at a small round table husband and wife set with other bride members, at another table were parents and friends. Dinner was served and the menu was outstanding also very good. We all dance to the music ,drink until early in the morning, the lights went out, after coming back on more dancing more done and lots of great fun was had but all, we left about 4:30 in the morning.

Sunday was a full day, Breakfast was also great, at this time the plan was to so into the museum downtown we were there for about four hours, what a museum this was like no other. After that of course it was time for dinner there was a very nice restaurant nearby were we all went to eat being there for some time enjoying our self. The time had for us to have some music for the day, which was a Ballet to see, this to me was very outstanding, very well put together, having wine and cheese with friends lots of laughter and talking, this was a great day, the weather was also good. We returning to the hotel and our room for the night, this was our last full day before leaving on Monday.

Monday, packing early before breakfast, we talk to our friends about the long weekend and a swell time for the both of us, also we went to the park which was two blocks from the hotel to take pictures. This park was full of status that you would not see back in states, head that stand from ground. We return to hotel for checking out, taking a cab to airport in the afternoon for home sweet home [smile)) arriving at home safe around 11pm. This was a great weekend, we had not been to Mexico City before, when asked to go to this wedding by friends our hearts jump for joy.

VISION

Sometime when I sat in church listening to the Mass loud and clear you beginning to think he is talking to me today. Miracle I have had and also vision that I have at some time in my life. Before I retired checking my breast one day found a lump [small] I went to see my doctor and we talk for a long time, he had his other doctor gave me a examination they both found the same thing in my left breast. My husband and I had just plain our vacation so I told my doctor and said when we get back if it still there we would talk, he answer was it will still be there [smile] I said miracle do happen? At the time my husband and I talk about it no one else knew about this. I was working in the computer room where they keep it very cold at all time because that was where the main frame computer was locate. I decide at that time I that this is a good for me to retired the years I had worked was thirty three years. After talking to my supervisor and telling him what my plans were, he was sad and so sorry that I would be leaving. Everyone was talking about what had happen, lots of Buzz, Buzz, from the noise coworkers the ones that did not talk to you at any time. The office gave me a nice retirement party, many supervisors and workers spoke great things of my service and I received some nice gifts. There were also coffee and sandwiches plus donuts, this so nice. After leaving my husband and I went on our vacation for a week at the Cape. [mass].

VISION

When we returned for our vacation I went back to my doctor to see what had happen, things were the same he told me I had cancer in the left breast. He also told me what cancer doctor I must see one that he knew and was very good. I went to see him we talk for a while, also taking x-rays tell me what I should do. I had to go six months for chemotherapy, my husband was very supposed of me when I went to see the doctor for my treatment he could come in the office with me. When I didn't understand what was going he would ask the questions.

I call and talk to my pastor I told him what had happen and understand what was going on, he begin to pray with me over the phone for a while, after ward I thank him for being there for me. I fell asleep, as I sleep there were many dreams like miracle things, angles I saw and voices that I had not experience before also lights. When I wake up the next morning my faith told me everything would be all right, I also felt like I was born again in Christ aman.

The operation went very well, I had to have a mastectomy. God is so good and my best friend he is always there when I need him, this year is my twenty first year thank god.

Each month after that I had to see my specialist. Each year the cancer foundation had a meeting and luncheon for everyone in Atlantic City where several speakers talk about what had happen to people in the past years. This was good information for me because I meet people and we shared our stories.

INSPIRATION

Angles are always around me.
Compassion
Having faith: let others know there are better choices. life
There was a priest in my life at one time, he always
spoke so wonderful about religious life and the
Sacredness of human life. I have great memory of him
because he help me when my husband pass.
Faith
When I found out that I had breast cancer I didn't know
what was going to happen, my spiritually and
trust in God that whatever happen I would be
able to handle it no matter how difficult
Within six months the power of pray, angles, my pastor,
priest and husband was with me every day.
Faith has carried me a long way, I call this strong.

CHAPTER THREE

My mother begin to come into my dreams at this time, I do not dream of her often she would say you go this trip.

June 2009 was time to travel international to relax and to see other family. The week very well, while I was there for some reason I felt that was the place for me to be. This man came in my life which I was not looking for, talk for hours, laughed a lot, one day when we meet he had a gift for me and I ask if could I could open it and when I did it beautiful, did not know if it was the time for a kiss or hug [smile]. He was a wonderful person, he took me to lunch one day and dinner one night and told me that I would be back which I had no plans at that to return. That was June, would you believe that September I return to stay in my Condo and he was my guest for a week and had wonderful time.

KNOWLEDGE

My mother died years ago but she came back into my life in a dream after the passing of my husband. There were many dreams I had that I must go way to the Bahamas for healing and some nurture in my life again also taken good care of myself [life and health as bodily beings]. Bahamas was a very good place to get the knowledge of truth and appreciation of beauty. In the dream my mother gave me that nurture and nature which was already in me. The gift was to go and help someone that really needed my holy spirit and at the same time to help myself. I went to the Bahamas and saw family members for two days, when traveling to time share vacation they gave you a free night of games and dinner to meet other guess that came in the same you arrived to have fun.

They also tell you the places like shopping, tours and restaurant like everyone can go in the evening, sometime I pass not to attend for me it was to be there to clear my head and do nothing; beach; read and eat when I wanted. What a great feeling to have after losing your husband from medical problems for three years.

Each morning I would have lunch on the beach after a chair plus two towels to put in the sun. One day while reading a book I had a visit from a gentleman he came over and we begin talking. This was the first time talking to a man about how I was feeling inside, we talk for hours.

He asked me if I had a friend and I said I have many friends. He was single and work every day as a fisherman also had his own boat. One day he brought lunch and we eat at the lunch stand on the beach. He also asked me out to dinner on Friday night after a long day of fishing. We had a wonderful dinner at this small restaurant nearby where I was staying.

One day he brought me a gift saying I have something for you. His smile was like a growing flower where joy and laughter ring, every day held special care and dreams were always to share. The gift was wrap nicely I was acting like a little girl; when I open it he had given me a large sea shell, surprise was not the word; I was amaze all I could say was Thanks. The week went very well my birthday is in august and I was saying what my plans were. He gave me his card that had his phone number on it and said I could call him anytime. I gave him my phone number and told him not to loss it because men do some crazy things. The week was coming to an end one I will not forget. I returned home feeling fanatic.

I beginning calling to see what was available to my surprise there was a townhouse with two bedrooms, two floor balcony up stairs down stairs laundry room, large kitchen and living room also a private pool/car port.

The plain was to meet at the town house when I arrived and check-in but he was not there. I call him and had happen they call him to work at the list minute. I inform the clerk the time he would be arriving. There was a very warm welcome when we did see each other. The things he brought for a week for cooking was great surprise. We went food shopping and brought what we needed and special things he wanted. Sunday went well he fix coffee early and brought it to me in bed he also made breakfast. What a way to begin my week. Going to the pool for a dip and setting there on the balcony talking about his life when he was growing up. His family was large and he also had to attend church with his mother and father like I did, not too much difference from the life I had as I grown up.

I told him about my medical problem years back and I thought it might make a difference the way I would be treated but it didn't. He was so understanding the way he look at me saying it would not take anything for me as a wonderful person. [I begin to think where have he had been].

I ask him what was the plans for the day his face gave the answer. For dinner we both share in the cooking it was so nice working together felt like we had known each other for a long time.

Once in a life time having such a great time having a person in my life like him that don't need a lot of things, I saw the change in him within days that to me was the meaning of being RICH.

The next day he had to work that was ok with me, I meet some people that came on the weekend. We by the pool for a while and after they left I begin to read a book.

The moon we would talk about how the people would go crazy, drinking and driving fast. Some time we see the full moon clear as we would be by the water at night and seeing the moon in the water. He would say baby that is a beautiful thing you and I walking near ocean to night under the full moon.

Among the full moon there is all ways stars so bright and the sky is clear, it can be cold depend on where you are locate and the time of the year. The sky above us was beautiful with clouds on one side. For almost a minute we stood there looking at this since taking it all in.

There were many things I enjoy being away and that was one of them. The full moon is out for three night or four nights before becomes really full. The weather was 75' being with your love one what else would I want? Mable a glass of wine, Jack Daniel and a glass of beer for him? This was our birthday present to us. We were both born under the same sign. To think two earth people together.

We were on the balcony outside of our condo the world was ours and there was warm air over our faces. We were location at the end of the coral reef which also made us feel to enjoy the minute. This was late in the evening he [John] look up and saw a rainbow saying baby look there is a double rainbow there it was… no way I had never seen a double rainbow, there it was. One was strong and the other was weak but they were beautiful together. As he look up to the sky he also put his arms up as a cross as to say [Lord here I am]. Asking me if I was enjoying myself I said yes this is just what I need to be here with you [as I smile].

The next day we went to celebrate our birthday. We had dinner at a lovely club in the downtown area. The club had a stage for shows plus casino. The dinner was great as we were eating there was artiste singing and good music playing, after that was over it was time for the live show, as they say it's show time. Great dancing also an impression he was young and very good. The show was outstanding. The show lasted about an hour and half.

After leaving we decided to go and attend another club and party some more, we ran into some of his friends and the party begin… oh what fun we all had [fun]. He had a way of listening that let me know he really care. His smile made me feel right at home.

Harmony with other people some bring Faith in times of doubt and some bring Hope to me, some bring Love that casts out fear and sets my spirit free. With some I've laughed, with some I've danced, as Joy is theirs to give. From some I've learned of inner PEACE and a simpler way to live my wreath entwines the gifts of all the caring folks I know… I weave a ribbon of love around And tie it in a bow. From a friend…

Before leaving the Island my friend looked so sad but, handsome at the same time. I wanted to take him in my arms and never letting go. He also said that I would be back. After returning home from my great vacation, I received a call from him and left a message he sound so sexy over the phone. Calling him back that evening it was wonderful to hear his voice we talk for a while and said it would be great to see me again. Sunday night he called told him baby you can call me anytime day or night. We must be faith to whatever faith we hold. All through we came from two difference world we both believe in prayer before eating we would pray.

I was always a good listener and I would let him know how good he was as a person. He share his advice and experience gently. The next time we talk was about his birthday which is in September and wanted me to come back and celebrated which was cool because mine is in August. Talking to him every week for two months I begin plains to return to the island ,asking him if he would be my guest for a week in September to celebrated our birthday he said yes baby I would love too.

On Friday was my last full day our plan for dinner was big when John came home for work he brought fresh lobster tails. This was his thing to cook them for dinner and he was good at it. He was such a great cook and love doing it for his [baby] that is what he always called me. Potato salad, collard greens, rolls and beer was what we had. This was an outstanding evening we shared so beautiful together, we also begin to get a strong bond toward each other. I did not want to leave. I left for home on Saturday around noon he drove me to the airport and told me to make sure you call me when you get home. He said I don't care what time it will be, I will be waiting to hear from you. It was late when I return home and I call him to let him know I was home safe and thank him for a lovely week.

Young love is one thing but to love someone and have a strong bond between each other is something else. I knew when he had pains and would not be near each other and when we were together and things happen he also knew what I was thinking, there was that look plus a laugh. Faith is good to have all the time.

After my trip we talk about twice a week letting me know that was going on. He suggested we should see each other every year for our birthday, that would give me something to look forward to coming back to the Bahamas.

The loss of a parent is so hard… we would get a lot attention when we lose a parent then a year or two goes by and everyone forgets but you don't forget. This is what John [my friend] telling me about his mother that had passed about a few years before I meet him. He always talks about her. For me when I lost my father it took me years [4] before I would let go.

Returning home from that great week with my friend gave me more richness in my life. There was peace, joy, kindness that doesn't cost anything and patience which is the fruit of the spirit, each is one of a kind. Talking to him and listing to what he was saying he was so glad to have me in his life. He also said his mother wanted him to have a kind woman for him to enjoy.

I would all ways plan two trips a year to see him. The next year I started the year off being there to see the super bowl with him. Football was his game [raven] was his team and they were playing that Sunday. He never would nap on a game, but he did off and on then I would make noise and he would said what going on. From that I knew something was not right because at that time I begin to know him very well. After the game he told me he was not feeling good and was getting a cold so I let rest until dinner. On this trip we stay by the ocean [condo] often I awake to the sound of the ocean waves, there are so many beaches on the island so lovely and some are rock formation.

The times when I was there we would go sightseeing seeing places that I had not seen before like family with money, they all live in a special part of the island. This was great at this time of my life to find someone that enjoys the little things that both of us like. He gave me two more large ocean shell and they were more lovely than the first one, you can't understand what this means to me. We both love the water and the wisdom from above is first of all is pure. Driving along the ocean is one of the things I like doing plus sharing the stories of love and deception. One time we saw an older lady walking along the road we stop the car and park to talk with her she was eighty-five year old, this is how some of the older lady would get around they all look so good, we took her where she wanted to go that made me feel good. We did this often when we were out driving. He told me any place I wanted to go he would take me just let him know.

We had so much fun on Thursday night when we went to the club, by this time I know the fellows that work the bar they would say welcome back home. My friend said to them look at my lady, is she fine or what? We all laugh. I said gave me a yellow bird which is an island drink and they are good.

Let there be peace on earth and let it begin with me… let there be peace on earth, the peace that was meant to be. With God as our Father, brothers all are we; Let me walk with my brother in perfect harmony Let peace begin with me, let this be the moment now With every step I take, let this be my solemn vow… To take each moment and live each moment in peace eternally. Let there be peace on earth and let it begin with me.

He called me to say that he was going to his home island for some business for two weeks and to be with his sisters. He asked me to call him while he was there so I did. This was good for him because he needed to get away. When I talk to him everything was going on well. He had meet with some of his old friends and they had stay up all night until about five in the morning, his sister was going crazy not knowing where he was., they had a great time talking about times when they were young. He said as soon as things ended in court about their land, guess what I will be on the next plane back to Freeport I will call you after I return home.

May 2011 I choose this month to travel back to visited my great friend because I had a dream about him and it was not good after waking up in the middle of the night and wouldn't go back to sleep, I said to myself what is going. I call and told him that I was coming down, so he said for me to take a cab because he had work and could not pick me up for the airport.

This week was great and wonderful but there feeling which I didn't have before something was wrong and he said everything was all right didn't question anything just listening. We drove to the ocean he didn't speak and I wondered why the silence at this I could tell he had something on his mind. We were then overlooking the ocean he parked the car and turn to me looking me in the eye saying his son wanted him to move to Nassau or moving back home with his sisters which he didn't because his sisters was a mess. He loved living in Freeport because this was where he worked and all his fishing friends were there for him I could understood what he was going thought. I begin to read between the lines that he was very sick so I ask him what are you going to do I am going to stay In Freeport. I was glad I had come down that month. We still was planning to see each other on birthday in September. In my heart I just wanted to see in May because of the dream I had early, this was the close bond and feeling I had with him from the very beginning.

The Lord is my shepherd: I shall not want. He maketh me to lie down in green pastures: he leadeth me beside the still waters. He Restoreth my soil: he leadeth me in the paths of righteousness for his name's sake. Yea though I walk through the valley of the shadow of death. I will fear no evil : for thou art with me: thy rod and thy staff they comfort me. Thou prepares a table before me in the presence of mine enemies: thou anointest my head with oil : my cup runneth over. Surely goodness and mercy shall follow me all the days of my life: and I will dwell in the house of the Lord forever.

Psalm 23

Sometime life throws us curbs and what we do is run them out with God beside us. My mother in the dream I had of her early on know he was sick and wanted me to be there to give him as much joy and pray for him each day. He had a remarkable way of showing his thanks, also a great feeling of love about him at any time. What is so great having someone in your life to enjoy one day at a time, planning small things as to visited friends ,setting by the ocean, watching the sun set and rise. We would talk and laugh about silly things. I just love hearing him laugh and the look he would have on his face.

I will not forget what he would all way said please don't give up on me that something I would never do. Leaving in May he took me the airport to return home this was hardest thing for me to do. I begin to cry the hug was tight and long and the kiss was like no other. After I got home that night I call to let him know I was home safe. The next question was… what was that hug all about [smile] he said did you get that too. I love you and this gift I leave with you. We talk many times after that more than before. The last time we talk he was saying that he could hardly stand up and was so sick. Every day I would pray for him, than one night late I call and this young lady answer the phone and I ask who she was, she said I have been trying to reach you. I am John granddaughter he passes away. I could not talk to her I became so nervous I told her I would call the next day. When I got off the phone I had to have a drink of wine I would not sleep. I did talk to her the next night for a long and she told me I was at the top of his list she also told me to come when I was ready. The rest of the month was very hard for me around the time of his birthday in my dream he gave me a visited to show me all the good times we shaved. There were many angles everywhere, for about three to four months he would visit. I miss him deadly. The next year I went back and meet his granddaughter and talk to his grandson they were so nice I also had lunch with his granddaughter, it was fun. While I was there his best friend and his friend that he works with got to see each other and told me about this last days. I went to his boat and got the last sea shell that he had gotten his friend that work with said he would wanted me to have them. He told me not to close that book? After dreaming about him and his last visited with the angles this was so deep could not explain how I felt when waking up.

Someone once said it's best to have loved and lost to have never loved at all. I am so much of a better person now know matter there you go and how many people you meet they all have some of the same problems. Make sure you listen to what they are saying before you answer.

Part of the Irish blessing

May the road rise to meet you
May the wind be always at your back
May the warm rays of sun fall upon your home and
may the hand of a friend always be near.